11+
MATHEMATICS

Series editor Tracey Phelps,
the 11+ tutor with a

96% PASS RATE

Ages 10–11

Practice

SCHOLASTIC

Published in the UK by Scholastic, 2020

Book End, Range Road, Witney, Oxfordshire, OX29 0YD

Scholastic Ireland, 89E Lagan Road, Dublin Industrial Estate, Glasnevin, Dublin, D11 HP5F

www.scholastic.co.uk

1 2 3 4 5 6 7 8 9 1 2 3 4 5 6 7 8 9 0

A CIP catalogue record for this book is available from the British Library.

ISBN 978-1407-18379-4

Printed and bound by Replika Press Pvt. Ltd.

Paper made from wood grown in sustainable forests and other controlled sources.

Authors

Tracey Phelps, Paul Hollin

Editorial team

Rachel Morgan, Vicki Yates, Christine Bruce

Design team

Dipa Mistry, Couper Street Type Co.

Illustrations

Tracey Phelps

P59 Thai baht icon made by Freepik from www.flaticon.com

Contents

About the CEM test

About the CEM test

The Centre for Evaluation and Monitoring (CEM) is one of the leading providers of the tests that grammar schools use in selecting students at 11+. The CEM test assesses a student's ability in Verbal Reasoning, Non-verbal Reasoning, English and Mathematics. Pupils typically take the CEM test at the start of Year 6.

Students answer multiple-choice questions and record their answers on a separate answer sheet. This answer sheet is then marked via OMR (Optical Mark Recognition) scanning technology.

The content and question type may vary slightly each year. The English and Verbal Reasoning components have included synonyms, antonyms, word associations, shuffled sentences, cloze (gap fill) passages and comprehension questions.

The Mathematics and Non-verbal Reasoning components span the Key Stage 2 Mathematics curriculum, with emphasis on worded problems. It is useful to note that the CEM test may include Mathematics topics which students will be introduced to in Year 6, such as ratio, proportion and probability.

The other main provider of such tests is GL Assessment. The GLA test assesses the same subjects as the CEM test and uses a multiple-choice format.

About this book

Scholastic 11+ Maths for the CEM Test is part of the Pass Your 11+ series and offers authentic practice activities. This book offers:

- Targeted practice and opportunities for children to test their understanding and develop their mathematical skills.
- Opportunities for children to master different question styles on key 11+ maths topics including time, ratio, geometry, algebra, probability and much more.
- Includes a mix of practice and assessment.
- Short answers at the end of the book.
- Extended answers online with useful explanations at www.scholastic.co.uk/ pass-your-11-plus/extras or via the QR code opposite.

Instructions for completing the tests in this book

For each of the questions in the book, write the correct answer in the answer lozenge, or for multiple choice questions write the correct letter.

Example question:

Which of the following numbers is divisible by exactly 6?

A	B	C	D	E
374	616	174	452	259

C

Properties of numbers

1   Alisha's teacher asks her to start at 145 and counts four steps of 10. She stops at 185.

For the second task, she has to start at 3217 and count seven steps of 100.

Where will she stop?

_____

2   Tom is practising reading large numbers. He looks at the number 9,742,683.

How many hundreds of thousands does it have?

_____ hundred thousand

3   If these five numbers are placed in order from smallest to largest, which number will be in the middle?

| 32,830 | 24,083 | 29,471 | 31,426 | 34,825 |

A	B	C	D	E
Thirty-two thousand, eight hundred and thirty	Twenty-four thousand, and eighty-three	Twenty-nine thousand, four hundred and seventy-one	Thirty-one thousand, four hundred and twenty-six	Thirty-four thousand, eight hundred and twenty-five

_____

4   Class 6 are comparing the populations of Nottingham and Leicester.

City population: Nottingham 729,977   Leicester 492,916

To estimate the difference in population between the two cities they round each population to the nearest hundred thousand, then subtract one from the other. How many hundreds of thousand is the estimated population difference between Nottingham and Leicester?

_____ hundred thousand

5   Kelvin thinks of a number. He says it is an even number that can be divided by three with no remainder. It is greater than 20 but less than 30.

What is Kelvin's number?

_____

6 Gregory lives in a cold country. One morning the temperature is −4°C. He puts the central heating on and the temperature goes up by 7°C.

Later on, he turns the heating off and the temperature goes down by 5°C. What will the temperature be now?

( ) °C

7 Two hours before the start of a football cup final, there are 23,000 supporters inside the football stadium.

For the next two hours, 1000 supporters arrive every quarter of an hour.

How many supporters will be watching at kick off?

( ) supporters

8 Laura writes a sequence. What will be the next number in her sequence?

5   11   23   47 …

( )

9 Jamal is measuring temperature changes.

At 6pm the temperature outside is 5°C.

If the temperature drops by 2°C every hour, what will the temperature outside be at midnight?

( ) °C

10 Jasmine has to list all the factors of 40. She discovers only one of these is both odd and prime.

Which number is it?

( )

11 Which of the numbers below is exactly one hundred thousand less than this number: seven million, four hundred and seventy-five thousand, three hundred and eighty-two?

A	B	C	D	E
7,375,382	6,475,382	7,465,382	7,474,382	7,375,282

( )

/11

Addition and subtraction

1 46,325 + 53,675 = 100,000

What does 200,000 − 53,675 equal?

⬭

2 A farmer grows different vegetables. He has 5600 potatoes in one field, 7300 onions in another and 4300 parsnips in a third field.

If he saves 200 of each vegetable for his village, how many vegetables altogether will he have left to sell?

⬭ vegetables

3 Which one number can be used to make both of these calculations correct.

624 − _____ = 390   _____ + 176 = 410

A	B	C	D	E
424	276	234	300	200

⬭

4 Anna goes to her local fruit shop. She buys an orange for 20p, an apple for 15p, a grapefruit for 30p and a banana for 25p.

How much change will she receive from £1?

 p

5 If 243 − 165 = 78

What is 165,000 + 78,000?

6 Find the missing number in this addition.

```
    2 5 8
    3 0 5
    4 8 2
+   * * *
  ─────────
  1 3 7 8
```

⬭

7 Wendy and Peter's parents decide to move house. They sell their house for £143,000 and buy a smaller house for £121,500. They also have to pay fees of £3725.

How much money will they have left over?

£ _____ . ____

8 Estimate the answer to this calculation to the nearest hundred thousand.

628,479 + 489,201 + 250,382

_____

9 A zookeeper weighs five different animals one day. She makes a note of their masses.

Animal	Elephant	Lion	Giraffe	Rhino	Hyena
Mass (kg)	5400	170	820	2200	52

How much heavier is an elephant than all the other animals put together?

_____ kg

10 The population of a small town has 12,382 women, 11,416 men, 5130 girls and 3950 boys.

How many more females than males are there?

_____

11 This chart shows the world's six tallest buildings:

	Building	Country	Height (feet)
1	Burj Khalifa	United Arab Emirates	2717
2	Shanghai Tower	China	2073
3	Abraj Al-Bait Tower	Saudi Arabia	1971
4	Ping An Finance Center	China	1965
5	Goldin Finance 117	China	1957
6	Lotte World Tower	South Korea	1891

Which tower is 182 feet taller than the Lotte World Tower?

_____

/11

Multiplication and division

1 Jim is reading a new book and is really enjoying it. He reads 15 pages a night for five nights, then 20 pages a night for three nights and is finished.

How many pages does the book have?

pages

2 $17 \times 24 = 408$

What will 34×24 be equal to?

A	B	C	D	E
666	786	808	816	832

3 A bag of 100 sweets is shared between 30 children. How many can they each be given so that they all get the same number of sweets?

sweets

4 The cost of theatre tickets is £9 for children and £16 for adults. For every three children's tickets that are bought, one adult ticket is free.

How much would the tickets for a group of five children and two adults cost?

£ .

5 A teacher has 180 sheets of paper. She gives 12 sheets each to 12 children, and splits the remainder into two equal piles.

How many sheets of paper will be in each pile?

sheets of paper

6 Hanmo thinks of a number. She says the difference between the number squared and the number cubed is 48.

Which number is she thinking of?

7 A school of 420 children is divided equally between 15 classes.

How many children will there be in each class?

(children)

---

8 Two numbers less than 30 both have 5 as a factor. Multiplying the two numbers together gives 375.

What is the smaller of the two numbers?

( )

---

9 600 people each donate £25 to an animal charity. The charity gives two thirds to a dogs' home, and one third to a cats' home.

How much will the cats' home receive?

(£   .)

---

10 A textiles shop cuts a large roll of fabric into identical 2-metre lengths. They charge £10 per 2-metre length of fabric, and sell them all for a total of £500.

How long was the original roll of fabric?

(m)

11
| Information: Using decimal rates: 1 megabyte = 1000 kilobytes (kb) |
| 1 gigabyte = 1000 megabytes (mb) |

How many kilobytes does a 64-gigabyte memory stick hold?

A	B	C	D	E
64,000kb	640,000kb	6,400,000kb	64,000,000kb	640,000,000kb

( )

/11

Time

1 Robert is roasting a chicken which needs to be cooked for 30 minutes per kilo plus an extra 20 minutes. The chicken weighs 2.5kg. Robert puts the chicken in the oven at 11:45.

At what time will the chicken be ready?

(___ : ___)

2 Archie was born at 15:30 on 1st May. His sister, Poppy, was born exactly 14 months earlier.

On which date does Poppy celebrate her birthday?

(___)

3 What is three quarters of an hour minus 7 minutes?

A	B	C	D	E
27 minutes	38 minutes	43 minutes	31 minutes	28 minutes

(___)

4 Look at the timetable for diving lessons below. Kieran attends the advanced class every Monday, Wednesday and Friday. How much time does Kieran spend at diving classes every week?

Lesson	Start time	Finish time
Beginners	15:45	16:10
Intermediate	16:20	16:55
Advanced	17:50	18:40

(___ hours ___ minutes)

5 Annie's watch is showing 14:03, but it is slow by 17 minutes.

What is the correct time?

(___ : ___)

6 Tessa arrives at her office at 08:40 and works until 10:55, when she has a ten-minute coffee break. She takes a 50 minute lunch break at 13:10 and stops at 15:40 for a five-minute tea break. Tessa leaves work at 17:15.

How many hours and minutes has Tessa spent working at her desk?

(___ hours ___ minutes)

7

On 21st December, the sun rises at 08:08 and sets at 15:40.

How many hours and minutes of daylight are there
altogether on this date?

(hours   minutes)

8

Below is a timetable showing coach services running between Liverpool and Leeds.

Liverpool	06:45	07:12	08:35
Salford Quays	08:10	08:48	10:08
Manchester	08:30	09:19	10:34
Chadderton	09:40	10:34	11:49
Leeds	10:30	11:30	12:48

How long does the slowest coach journey from
Liverpool to Leeds take?

(hours   minutes)

9

Below is part of a calendar for February in a leap year.

On which date will the third Thursday in March fall?

February

Mon	Tue	Wed	Thu	Fri	Sat	Sun
1	2	3	4	5	6	7
8	9	10	11	12	13	14
15	16	17	18	19	20	21
22	23					

(   )

10

A coffee shop opens daily from 09:30 to 17:00 on weekdays and from 08:30 until
18:00 on Saturdays and Sundays.

For how many hours is the coffee shop open for
business in a fortnight?

(hours)

11

Bianca spends 25 minutes every evening after school practising her piano. How long does
she spend practising in a week?

A	B	C	D	E
2 hours and 5 minutes	1 hour and 55 minutes	2 hours	2 hours and 10 minutes	2 hours and 15 minutes

(   )

/11

Money 1

1 Sam wants to buy a magazine costing £2.99. He wants to give the shopkeeper the exact money. What is the smallest number of coins Sam can pay with?

| coins |

2 Florrie is having a birthday party and wants to buy some balloons. She has £10.00 to spend. She buys a balloon pump for £2.00 and spends the rest on balloons costing 25p per pack.

How many packs of balloons can she buy?

| packs |

3 A school secretary orders 45 exercise books costing 55p each and 45 notebooks costing 45p each.

How much will the total order cost?

A	B	C	D	E
£90.00	£72.45	£68.50	£135.00	£45.00

4 Zac has a shopping list with the following items.

pasta	£1.49	coffee	£3.75
bread	£2.10	cheese	£4.20
olive oil	£2.99	orange juice	£1.85
butter	£2.10		

Zac pays with a £20 note. How much change will he receive?

£ .

5 Harriet has two separate savings accounts containing a total of £312.00. There is £48.00 more in one account than the other.

How much money does Harriet have in her larger savings account?

£ .

6   A total of £1.26 is made up of equal numbers of 1p coins, 2p coins, 5p coins and 10p coins.

How many coins are there in total?

(coins)

---

7   Chammi and Nihal and their two children stay at a hotel in London for four nights. They pay £300 per night for a family suite. The family all have breakfast in the hotel's restaurant each morning of their stay – an adult's breakfast costs £10.25 and a child's breakfast costs £6.25.

How much was the total bill for the hotel?

(£   .   )

---

8   Dan decides to join his local gym. Membership is priced at £30 per month, and Dan will be able use all the facilities. If he pays for a year in advance, he will get a 30% discount.

How much will Dan have to pay if he chooses to pay for his annual membership in advance?

(£   .   )

---

9   Adele, her sister and her brother do some household chores so their mother gives them £12.00 to share equally between them. Adele also mows the lawn and is given £5.00 for this.

How much has Adele earned for her chores?

(£   .   )

---

10   Owen buys his lunch at a motorway service station. He buys two cheese and tomato rolls costing £2.99 each, a cereal bar costing 99p and a bottle of orange juice costing £1.49.

Owen pays with a £10 note. How much change will he receive?

A	B	C	D	E
£1.44	£1.54	£1.64	£2.54	£2.44

(   )

/10

Money 2

1 | Information: $1 US dollar = 75p (UK £)

Vidhya visits New York to stay with her sister. While she is there, she buys herself a new coat costing $90.00.

What is the cost of Vidhya's new coat in British pounds?

£ _____ . ____

---

2 | Information: £1 UK = $1.9 Australian dollars

Marina and Peter have been looking at buying a holiday home and have decided to buy a house in Sydney, Australia. The house is priced at $380,000 Australian dollars.

How much is the house in British pounds?

£ _____ . ____

---

3 | Information: $1 Canadian dollar = 60p (UK £)

Jack buys a new winter coat for £90.00 before flying out to Canada on holiday. On his arrival in Toronto, he sees the exact same coat priced at $90.00.

How much could Jack have saved if he had bought his coat in Toronto?

A	B	C	D	E
£54.00	£36.00	£18.00	£27.00	£46.00

(_____)

---

4 | Information: £1 UK = £20 Egyptian pounds

Henry is interested in Ancient Egypt and has flown out to Giza to visit the Great Pyramids. He has exchanged £300 British pounds for Egyptian pounds.

How many Egyptian pounds will Henry receive?

(_____ Egyptian pounds)

---

5 | Information: €1 Euro = 80p (UK £)

On their holiday in Paris, Mr and Mrs Jones and their nine-year-old twins visit the Louvre to see the *Mona Lisa*. Tickets cost €40.00 each for adults and €15.00 each for children.

How much are tickets for the whole family in British pounds?

£ _____ . ____

6 | Information: $1 Canadian dollar = 60p (UK £)

Aimie and Adrian travel to Canada for their honeymoon. They hire a car and drive around sightseeing for two days. When they refuel the car, the bill comes to $70.

How much is this in British pounds?

£ ___ . ___

---

7 | Information: ₹1 Indian rupee = 1p (UK £)

Erika travels to Kerala in India to visit her grandparents. When she books her return flight, it costs ₹52,540.

How much does Erika's flight home cost in British pounds?

₹ ___ . ___

---

8 | Information: £1 UK = ¥150 Japanese yen

Jamal and Nadia decide to celebrate the New Year in Tokyo, Japan. They exchange £500 cash for Japanese yen prior to their trip.

How many Japanese yen do they take with them for spending?

¥ ___ . ___

---

9 | Information: ₺1 Turkish lira = 12p (UK £)

Ritchie returns from a fortnight in Turkey with several gifts for his family. He has spent ₺2400 Turkish lira on clothes and ₺3600 Turkish lira on perfume.

How much has Ritchie spent in total in British pounds?

₺ ___ . ___

---

10 | Information: £1 UK = $1.30 US dollars

David has been to New York on business and has decided to stay another night to watch a basketball match. Tickets to the match cost $260 each.

How much does David's ticket cost in British pounds?

A	B	C	D	E
£200.00	£180.00	£240.00	£210.00	£225.00

(___)

/10

Fractions

1 At a rugby match there is a total of 12,711 spectators. One third of the crowd are seated; the remainder have to stand to watch the match.

How many spectators are standing?

(_____ spectators)

---

2 There are 32 children in Mrs Edward's class and one quarter of her students are girls.

One day, half the boys are absent and all the girls are in school?
How many children are in her class that day?

(_____ children)

---

3 Grace, Kim and Henry share a sum of money between them. Henry gets one half of the total amount. Kim gets £20. Grace gets £4 less than Kim.

How much money does Henry get?

A	B	C	D	E
£72.00	£24.00	£28.00	£36.00	£48.00

(_____)

---

4 There are 100 children in a choir. Half of them are aged 7 and a quarter of them are aged 8. The remaining children are all 9 years old.

How many children are 9?

(_____ children)

---

5 In a ballooning competition there are 90 hot air balloons. One hour after the scheduled time to take off, two fifths of the balloons are still on the ground.

How many hot air balloons are in the air?

(_____ balloons)

---

6 Neil bought a large box of chocolates. There were 60 chocolates in the box. He ate a third of them on Sunday. Neil's brother found them and ate one fifth of the remaining chocolates on Tuesday. Neil's sister ate half of the remaining chocolates on Wednesday.

How many chocolates were left?

(_____ chocolates)

7 The mass of a fully loaded car is 1360kg. The mass of the people in the car is two fifths of the total mass.

What is the mass of the car without the people inside?

(⬭ kg)

8 Priya, Saskia and Millie club together to buy a present for their mother's birthday. The present costs £36. Priya contributes half of the money and Millie gives one third.

How much money does Saskia contribute?

(£ ⬭ .)

9 Julian's petrol tank has a capacity of 72 litres. Currently, his tank is $\frac{5}{8}$ full.

How many more litres are needed to fill the petrol tank?

(⬭ litres)

10 A basket contains 36 eggs. $\frac{1}{6}$ are broken and $\frac{1}{9}$ have gone off.

How many eggs are fine to eat?

(⬭ eggs)

11 Lizz made 240 chocolate cupcakes to sell at her school fete. She sold one third of the cakes during the first hour of the fete. By midday, she had sold one quarter of the remaining cakes. By the end of the fete, she had sold two thirds of the remaining cakes.

How many cakes did Lizz have left?

(⬭ cakes)

12 A new coffee shop has hundreds of customers on its first day open for business. The coffee shop serves 168 coffees in the first hour. Seven twelfths of the coffees served are espresso. A quarter of the total number of coffees are lattes and the rest are Americanos.

How many Americanos are served?

A	B	C	D	E
28	98	42	58	24

(⬭)

/12

Decimals

1

Stephen tries to mark the point 0.68 on a number line.

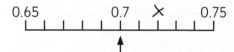

How far away is he from the correct answer?

(.)

2

A piece of string is 45cm long. Kevin cuts off 7.5cm from one end, and then cuts 2.7cm from the other end.

How long is the piece of string now?

(cm)

3

Trey calculates that 0.875 + 0.398 = 1.273.

Which is the correct inverse calculation to check if Trey is right?

A	B	C	D	E
0.398 + 0.875 = 1.273	0.875 − 0.398 = 1.273	1.273 + 0.398 = 0.875	1.273 − 0.398 = 0.875	3.98 + 8.75 = 12.73

( )

4

A fence-maker uses planks of wood that are 1.85m long and 0.15m wide. He stands them vertically, side by side, so that they are touching.

How long a fence can be made with 200 planks?

(m)

5

Information: 1 inch = 2.54cm

Gemma has three sticks. One is 2 inches long, one is 4 inches and the third is 5 inches.

If she puts the sticks end to end, what will be the total length in cm?

(. cm)

6 A protein snack has some nutritional information on the packet.

Saturated fats	Sugars	Fibre	Protein	Salt
3.95g	4.6g	8.0g	7.6g	0.36g

How much more protein than saturated fat is there?

(.   g)

---

7 A tree is blown over in a storm and taken to a factory to be used to make furniture.
A machine cuts the tree trunk into 1000 equal pieces.

If the tree weighed 735kg, how much will each piece weigh?

(.   kg)

---

8 Henry measures some rice to use in his family's evening meal. He decides to calculate how many grains of rice he will use. He reads online that a single grain of rice weighs 0.025g, and he uses 25g per person.

If there are 4 people in Henry's family,
how many grains of rice does he cook altogether?

(grains of rice)

---

9 | Information: 1 gallon = 8 pints   1 pint = 0.57 litres |

A dairy farmer puts her cows' milk into 1-gallon barrels before sending the barrels to the bottling plant.

One day she sends 5 barrels. How many litres of milk is this?

(.   litres)

---

10 A factory makes laptops. The mass of each laptop is 2.5kg. The laptops are loaded into large crates and sent overseas.

Each crate can hold a maximum mass of 500kg. How many laptops can each crate hold?

A	B	C	D	E
100 laptops	200 laptops	300 laptops	400 laptops	500 laptops

(   )

/10

Percentages

1 45% of the 800 students at Abbey Park school are boys.

How many are girls?

(_____ girls)

2 Joe has saved £15,000. This is half of the 10% deposit that he needs to buy his first apartment.

What is the price of the apartment?

(£ _____ . ___)

3 There is a total of 40 marbles in a jar. 20% of the marbles are green and 60% are blue. The remaining marbles are all yellow.

How many marbles are yellow?

A	B	C	D	E
12	10	6	4	8

(_____)

4 A maths test had 40 questions. Florrie got 95% correct.

How many questions did Florrie get wrong?

(_____ questions)

5 A large sports shop is trying to reduce its stock levels and is discounting all its sports footwear in a sale.

Joshua wants to buy a pair of trainers that were originally priced at £90.00, but are now reduced to £76.50.

By how many per cent have the sports shop reduced the trainers?

(_____ %)

6 Russell gets £15 pocket money each month. His parents agree to an increase of 40 % if Russell takes on some extra chores, including walking the family dog and washing the cars.

How much pocket money will Russell get each month after the increase?

£ _____ . ____

---

7 William bought six travel guide books. He advertised them for sale on an internet site, hoping to make a profit of at least 25%. William spent a total of £45 on the books and eventually sold them for a total of £54.

What percentage profit did William gain from the sale of the travel guides?

_____ %

---

8 The Cameron family have completed 15% of their 360 mile car journey to Cornwall.

How many more miles do they have to travel before they complete their journey?

_____ miles

---

9 At St Mary's Primary School, 20% of the students have school lunches every day. The remaining students all take a packed lunch to school with them daily. A total of 250 students attend St Mary's.

How many students take a packed lunch to school?

_____ students

---

10 Ejaz receives his annual bonus from work. He pays 80% of his bonus into his bank account and spends the remaining money on presents for his three children.

If Ejaz spends £640 on the children, how much was his bonus?

£ _____ . ____

---

11 There is a total of 1500 spectators at a local football match, 7% of whom are children.

How many spectators are children?

A	B	C	D	E
107	105	110	115	98

_____

/11

Ratio

1 The sizes of the three angles in a triangle are in the ratio 1:4:4.

How many degrees will the smallest angle measure?

(____ °)

2 Olive has a bag containing 50 sweets. She keeps five for herself and gives one third of the remaining sweets to her sister Flo. Olive shares the rest of the sweets between her friends, Tom and Sophie, in the ratio 6:4.

How many sweets does Sophie receive?

(____ sweets)

3 Farmer Morris has the following animals on his farm.

28 ducks   24 cows   40 sheep   36 pigs

What is the ratio of sheep to cows, in its simplest form?

A	B	C	D	E
10:6	8:5	5:3	3:2	4:3

(____)

4 Two athletes take part in a 2000-metre race around a 400-metre track. One of the runners is faster than their rival in the ratio of 3:2.

How far into the race will the slower runner be lapped by their faster opponent?

(____ m)

5 The prices of three different pairs of jeans are in the ratio 4:3:1.

The most expensive pair cost £60 and the cheapest pair cost £15.

How much do the third pair of jeans cost?

(£ ____ . ____)

6   What is the ratio of the number of sides of a square to the number of faces on a cube?

A	B	C	D	E
4:8	3:8	1:2	2:3	1:3

7   Kieran has a number of 20p and £1 coins in his pocket in the ratio 3:5. If Kieran has fifteen £1 coins, how much money does he have in total?

£   .

8   In Year 5 at Highfield Primary School, the ratio of girls to boys is 6:5. The total number of children in the year group is 66.

How many boys are there?

boys

9   Kiana's recipe for banana bread states that the ratio of sugar to flour needs to be 4:5.

If Kiana uses 100g of sugar, how many grams of flour will she need?

g

10   At the start of a week, a small bookshop had fiction and non-fiction books for sale in the ratio 2:3. The bookshop had 2265 books for sale in total. By the end of the week, 210 of the fiction books had been sold and 353 of the non-fiction books had been sold.

How many non-fiction books did the bookshop have left at the end of the week?

books

11   How many girls are there in a class of 32 children if the ratio of boys to girls is 3:1?

A	B	C	D	E
24	8	18	28	12

/11

Proportion

1 Six portions of fish and chips cost £48.60 altogether.

How much would two portions cost?

(£ _____ . ___)

---

2 In a florist's shop, they sell two bunches of roses to every three bunches of daffodils. If they sell 42 bunches of daffodils, how many bunches of roses are sold?

(_____ bunches)

---

3 In Robin's office, there are five laptops to every computer. If there are four computers, how many computers and laptops are there in total in Robin's office?

A	B	C	D	E
24	20	18	25	28

(_____)

---

4 This recipe makes 12 vanilla cupcakes.

110g butter
110g caster sugar
2 eggs

1 tsp vanilla extract
110g self-raising flour
2 tablespoons milk

How many grams of self-raising flour would you need if you were only going to make six cupcakes?

(_____ g)

---

5 There are 15 children having swimming lessons. For every two girls, there are three boys.

How many girls are present at the lesson?

(_____ girls)

---

6 A car plant manufactures 350 new vehicles every week. Three out of every seven vehicles produced are white; the rest are different colours.

How many white vehicles are being manufactured each week?

(_____ vehicles)

7 In a horse race at Ascot, one in every six racehorses is grey. There are 24 horses in the race. How many of the racehorses are grey?

racehorses

8 Clara uses these ingredients to make a chocolate and orange cake. The cake serves four people.

1 orange
100g plain chocolate
2 eggs
280g caster sugar

25g cocoa powder
250ml sunflower oil
250g plain flour

Clara wants to make another cake to serve six people.
How many eggs will Clara need for the second cake?

eggs

9 Sherlie's car uses 8 litres of fuel to travel 50km.

How much fuel would Sherlie use if she were to drive 225km
on a journey to Manchester?

litres

10 A painter is preparing to repaint all the interior walls of a customer's house.

In order to create the correct colour, he needs to carefully blend one part 'Midnight Blue' to four parts 'Champagne'.

If the painter mixes 10 litres of paint in total, how much
'Midnight Blue' will he have used?

litres

11 Daniel has a recipe for fish pie that serves four people and requires 300g of smoked haddock.

How many grams of smoked haddock would be needed to make a
larger pie serving six people?

g

12 Lucy can read two pages in her reading book in 5 minutes and 12 seconds.

How long will it take her to read 20 pages?

A	B	C	D	E
50 minutes	52 minutes	54 minutes	56 minutes	108 minutes

/12

Probability

1 Yusef rolls a dice. What is the probability that he rolls a number less than 5?

Give your answer in its simplest form.

( ) in ( )

---

2 A bag contains 24 red marbles and 11 yellow marbles.
How many yellow marbles must be added to the bag to
make an even chance of taking a red marble out at random?

(yellow marbles)

---

3 There are four kings in a pack of 52 standard playing cards. What is the probability of
dealing a king when you deal the first card?

A	B	C	D	E
2 in 52	1 in 13	3 in 38	2 in 13	1 in 2

( )

---

4 Dinah and Adam count the cars passing the school gates and make a note of their colours.
They make a table of their results.

Colour	Red	Blue	Black	White
Number	2	3	7	4

What was the probability that a car was blue or black?
Give your answer in its simplest form.

( ) in ( )

---

5 A bag contains 15 coloured counters. There is a 1 in 5 chance of picking a blue counter.

How many counters are not blue?

(counters)

---

6 It is Josiah's birthday. He has a bag of assorted chocolates to share with his class. There are
seven caramels in the bag, and the probability of the first person getting a caramel is 1 in 5.

How many chocolates are there in the bag altogether?

(chocolates)

7 Tina's dad has eight white handkerchiefs, three blue ones, one black one and some red handkerchiefs. One morning, he pulls a handkerchief at random from his drawer.

If there is a 4 in 7 chance that he will pull a white handkerchief from the drawer, how many red handkerchiefs must he have?

( ) red handkerchiefs

---

8 A baker puts three cherries on top of each of the cakes she makes. She bakes 50 cakes, and by mistake puts only two cherries on top of five of the cakes.

What is the probability that her first customer will get a cake with three cherries on top?

( ) in ( )

---

9 A bag of 60 colour beads has 15 each of blue, red, yellow and green beads. Henry picks a bead at random from the bag.

What is the probability that it is not blue?
Give your answer in its simplest form.

( ) in ( )

---

10 Jess has a box of building blocks. She has 20 orange, 15 purple and 17 brown blocks. She closes her eyes and picks a single block out of the bag.

What is the probability that it is orange?
Give your answer in its simplest form.

( ) in ( )

---

11 There are 24 children in class 6C. The teacher chooses a child at random each day to take the register. If the probability of choosing a girl is 7 in 12, how many boys are there in the class?

A	B	C	D	E
12	11	10	9	8

( )

/11

Area and perimeter

1 How many square 50cm tiles will be needed to tile a kitchen floor measuring 8 metres long and 4 metres wide?

| | tiles |

2 Calculate the area of the compound shape to the right.

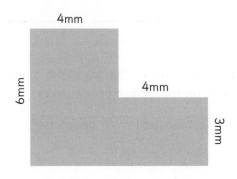

| | mm² |

3 A rectangle has an area of 480cm². One of its sides measures 12cm. What is the perimeter of the rectangle?

A	B	C	D	E
102cm	104cm	94cm	98cm	90cm

| |

4 Jules wants to put some new paving slabs on his patio. The paving slabs that Jules has chosen measure 50cm by 50cm. The slabs come in boxes of 24.

How many boxes will Jules need to buy?

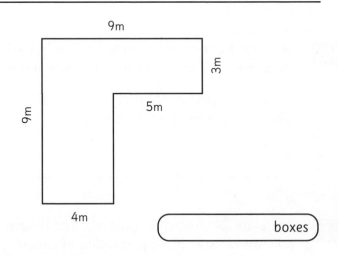

| | boxes |

5 What is the combined area of the two triangles below?

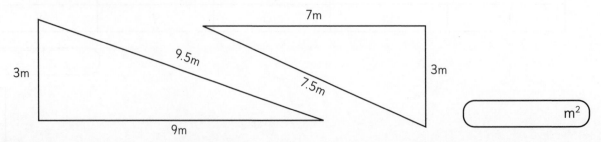

| | m² |

6 The length of Leila's living room is 1.5 times the width of the room.

If the room measures 6 metres wide, what is the area of the living room?

(m²)

---

7 What is the perimeter of the tennis court below?

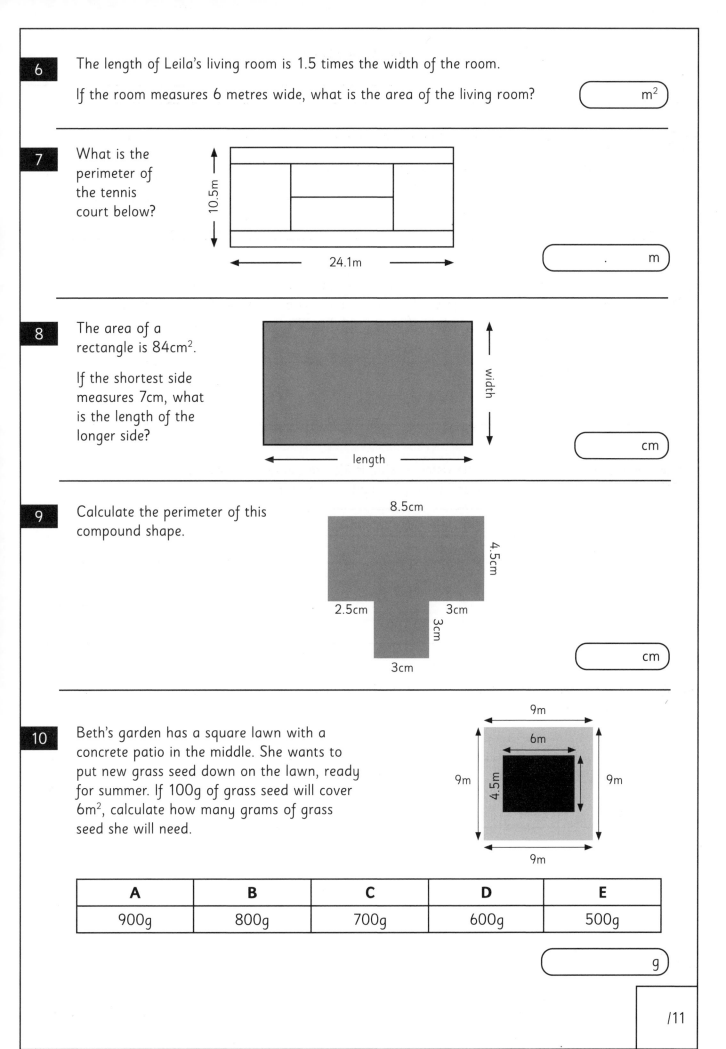

10.5m

24.1m

(. m)

---

8 The area of a rectangle is 84cm².

If the shortest side measures 7cm, what is the length of the longer side?

width

length

(cm)

---

9 Calculate the perimeter of this compound shape.

8.5cm

4.5cm

2.5cm   3cm

3cm

3cm

(cm)

---

10 Beth's garden has a square lawn with a concrete patio in the middle. She wants to put new grass seed down on the lawn, ready for summer. If 100g of grass seed will cover 6m², calculate how many grams of grass seed she will need.

9m

6m

9m   4.5m   9m

9m

A	B	C	D	E
900g	800g	700g	600g	500g

(g)

/11

Statistics

1   Sam's mean (average) score for four spelling tests is 30. The tests each had 50 questions.

What was Sam's score in her last spelling test, if her scores for the first three tests were 27, 25 and 24?

⬭

2   Three friends, Noah, Freddie and Lucy, are playing a board game together. The mean (average age of the three players is 9 years. The range of the three friends' ages is 5 years. The youngest player is Lucy, who is 6 years old. Freddie is the oldest player. The median of their ages is 10.

How old is Freddie?

⬭ years old

3   Rohan is 140cm tall. His little sister, Alisha, is 124cm tall and his older brother, Rishi, is 162cm tall. What is the mean (average) height of the children?

A	B	C	D	E
142cm	132cm	130cm	140cm	146cm

⬭ cm

4   The table below shows the amount of rainfall in millimetres recorded at a school in the first six months of the year.

What is the mean (average) rainfall in millimetres?

Month	January	February	March	April	May	June
Rain	12mm	25mm	38mm	43mm	22mm	16mm

⬭ mm

5   Joshua, Arun and Joe have a mean (average) age of 42.
Joshua is 38 and Arun is 45.

How old is Joe?

⬭ years old

6 The average (mean) temperature recorded over four days is 17°C. For three of the days, the temperatures were 16°C, 14°C and 18°C.

What was the temperature on the fourth day?

(_____ °C)

7 What is the median of the following set of numbers?

12, 8, 11, 7, 11, 13, 14, 12, 10

(_____)

8 The table below shows the summer and winter temperatures for four cities in Europe. What is the range in degrees Celsius for the temperature in summer and winter in Paris?

City	Summer	Winter
Manchester	17°C	– 4°C
Prague	20°C	– 5°C
Stockholm	12°C	– 8°C
Paris	18°C	– 3°C

(_____ °C)

9 The table below shows the finishing times of four children running in the 1km and 5km cross country races on sports day. The times are recorded in minutes and seconds. What is the range of finishing times for the 5k event?

Name	1k	5k
Nathan	8.44	40.30
Emma	7.45	39.18
Kieran	7.53	39.32
Olivia	8.54	42.40

(minutes _____ seconds)

10 What is the average (mean) finishing time for the 1k event?

(minutes _____ seconds)

11 What is the mode of the following set of numbers?

12, 13, 11, 12, 8, 6, 11, 6, 12, 11, 6, 12

A	B	C	D	E
6	11	10	12	13

(_____)

/11

Measurement

1

Information: 100cm = 1m   1000m = 1km

Peter travels to school by bus. The bus journey is 2.5km, and then he walks 200 metres to the school gate.

Peter calculates his total journey in centimetres. What is his answer?

$\boxed{\text{cm}}$

2

A farmer fills 6 sacks with potatoes. The total weight of the 6 sacks is 150kg.

If there are 100 potatoes in each sack, calculate the average weight of a potato in grams.

$\boxed{\text{g}}$

3

A barrel contains 8 litres of water. There are four holes in the bottom of the barrel, and each hole loses 40cl of water every hour. How long will it take for the all the water to drain from the barrel?

Information: 100 centilitres (cl) = 1 litre

A	B	C	D	E
50 minutes	3 hours	4 hours 20 minutes	6.5 hours	5 hours

$\boxed{}$

4

Calculate how many seconds there are in 15 hours.

$\boxed{\text{seconds}}$

5

Raheed uses the graph to estimate how many miles there are in 120km. What is his answer?

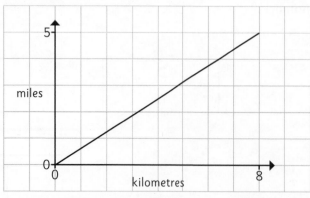

$\boxed{\text{miles}}$

6 | Information: 1kg = 2.2 lbs (pounds mass)

A class are weighing different rocks. Maria and Ross weigh a large rock twice, once on digital scales and once on some old balance scales. The digital scales tell them the rock has a mass of 4.5kg, and the balance scales tell them it has a mass of 10.3lb.

What is the difference in pounds between the two measurements?　　　(　　.　　 lbs)

---

7 | Liam has 12 paper cups, a jug and a bowl full of water. Using the bowl of water, he fills the 12 cups and the jug, and still has 300ml of water left over in the bowl.

If each cup has a capacity of 100ml and the jug holds 1.5 litres, what is the capacity of the bowl?

Information: 1 litre = 1000ml　　　(　　 litres)

---

8 | How many cubes with sides measuring 2cm could you fit into the shape below?

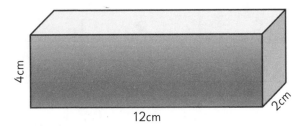

4cm

12cm

2cm

(　　 cubes)

---

9 | A teacher does an experiment with her class. She places a block of ice outside the classroom, and then they time how long it takes to melt. The block had a mass of 35kg at the beginning. The class estimates that it melts at the rate of 200g per hour.

How long will it take the block of ice to melt completely?

(　　 hours)

---

10 | The formula for calculating the volume of a pyramid is:
$\frac{1}{3}$ × the area of the base × the vertical height

Katie makes two identical modelling clay pyramids the size shown. How much modelling clay does she use?

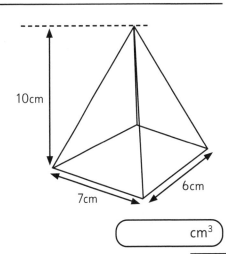

10cm

7cm

6cm

A	B	C	D	E
140cm³	280cm³	240cm³	320cm³	360cm³

(　　 cm³)

/10

Speed, distance and time

1 James took part in a race covering 21 miles. He completed the race in exactly 3 hours and 30 minutes.

What was James' average speed, in miles per hour?

> mph

2 A plane flying from London to Dubai completed the flight in 6 hours. The plane travelled at an average speed of 560 miles per hour.

What is the distance from London to Dubai?

> miles

3 How long will it take to travel 80 miles if your average speed is 50mph?

A	B	C	D	E
1 hour 36 minutes	1 hour 20 minutes	1 hour 24 minutes	1 hour 25 minutes	1 hour 12 minutes

> ___

4 Here is a map of a campsite.

What is the shortest distance between the cafe and the car park?

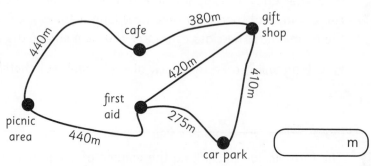

> m

5 Nadia ran 300 metres in 50 seconds.

What was her sprinting speed in metres per second?

> metres per second

6 Tom walks at a speed of 3km per hour. His sister, Jen, walks at 4km per hour. They both leave school at the same time and walk 2km to their house.

How many minutes will Tom arrive after Jen?

> minutes

7 The chart shows the approximate distances in miles between four capital cities. For example, the distance from Rome to London is 900 miles.

	Budapest	London	Rome	Reykjavik
Budapest		1000	500	1800
London	1000		900	1200
Rome	500	900		2000
Reykjavik	1800	1200	2000	

An aeroplane flies at 250 miles per hour. How long would it take to fly from Budapest to London?

(hours)

8 A train travelling at an average speed of 110 kilometres per hour takes 6 hours to complete its journey from London to Edinburgh.

What is the distance between the two cities, in kilometres?

(km)

9 If Harry runs at 4 metres per second, how long will it take him to complete one lap of the pitch?

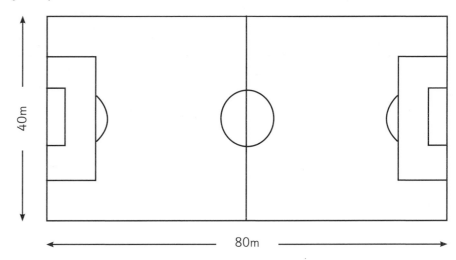

40m

80m

(seconds)

10 How long would it take a car travelling at 45mph to cover 30 miles?

A	B	C	D	E
25 minutes	30 minutes	15 minutes	45 minutes	40 minutes

( )

/10

Geometry 1

1 In an isosceles triangle, the two angles that are identical measure 50° each. How many degrees will the remaining angle measure?

°

2 Calculate the size of the missing angle in this triangle.

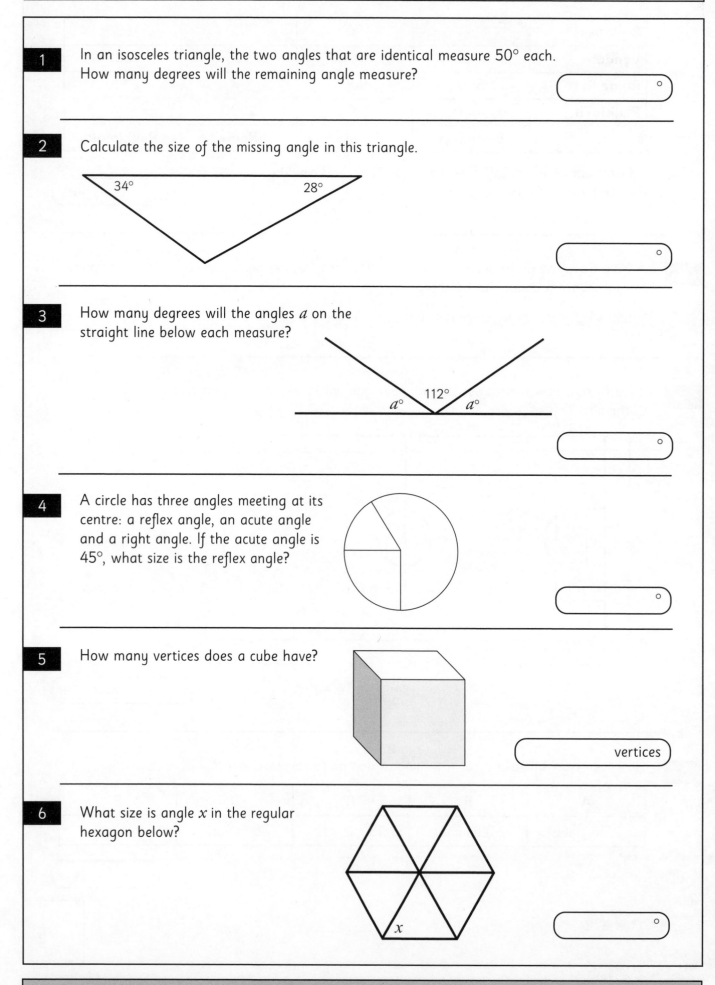

34°   28°

°

3 How many degrees will the angles a on the straight line below each measure?

112°

$a°$ $a°$

°

4 A circle has three angles meeting at its centre: a reflex angle, an acute angle and a right angle. If the acute angle is 45°, what size is the reflex angle?

°

5 How many vertices does a cube have?

vertices

6 What size is angle x in the regular hexagon below?

x

°

7   What is the obtuse angle between the hour hand and the minute hand on an analogue clock when the time is exactly 5 o'clock in the evening?

⬭ °

8   Hardeep draws a square with four identical circles inside. The sides of the square are each 48cm. What is the radius of each of the circles?

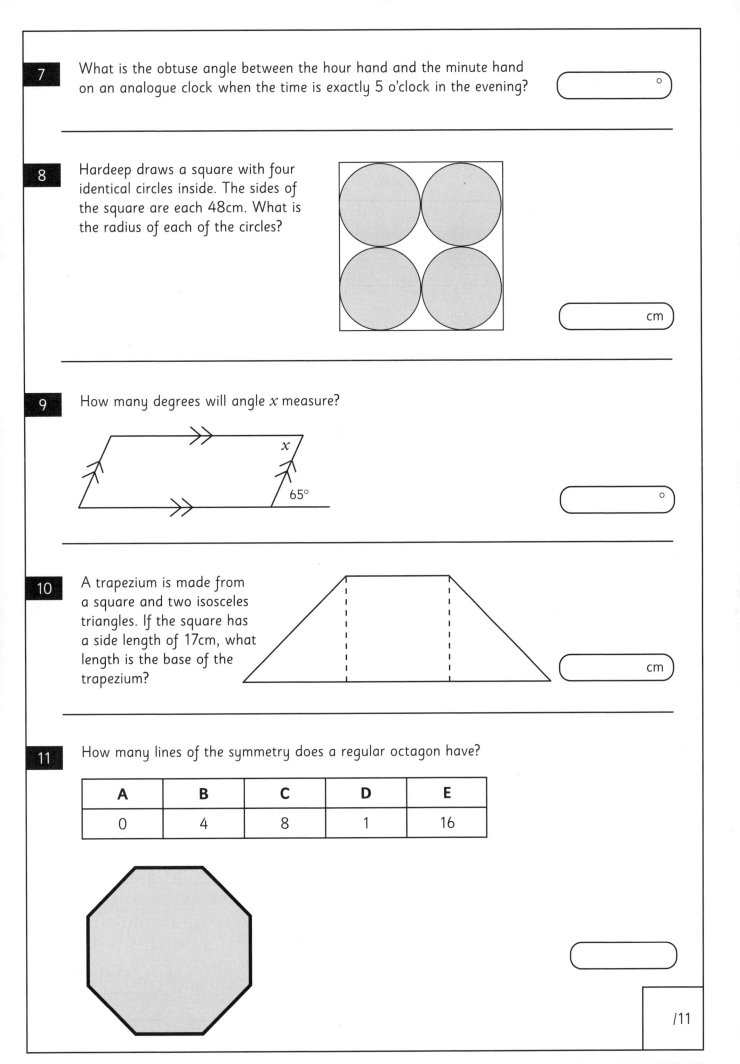

⬭ cm

9   How many degrees will angle x measure?

x

65°

⬭ °

10   A trapezium is made from a square and two isosceles triangles. If the square has a side length of 17cm, what length is the base of the trapezium?

⬭ cm

11   How many lines of the symmetry does a regular octagon have?

A	B	C	D	E
0	4	8	1	16

⬭

/11

Geometry 2

1 Cody writes down the names of of five quadrilaterals but he makes a mistake.

Parallelogram   Kite   Rhombus   Cuboid   Trapezium

Which one is incorrect?

2 How many degrees are there in the reflex angle between the hour hand and the minutes hand when the clock reads exactly 7 o'clock in the morning?

3 An equilateral triangle is cut out of a square. What is the size of angle c?

4 Shauna cuts a 70cm piece of wood into equal pieces to make a regular pentagon. There is no wood left over.

How long will each side of the pentagon be?

cm

5 In a right-angled triangle, angle a is twice as big as angle b. What is the size of angle b?

6 How many edges does a cube have?

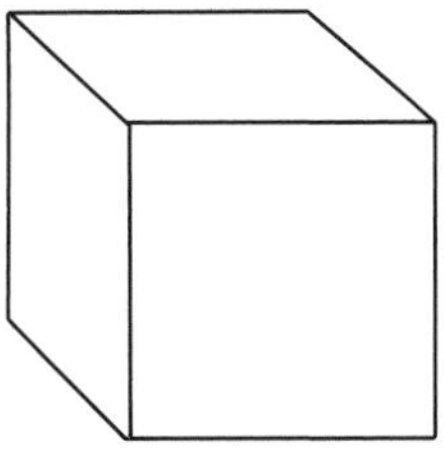

edges

7 Davina is making a net of a cube by sticking squares together. She needs to decide where to put the last square to make a correct net. Which one of the five sides shown will work?

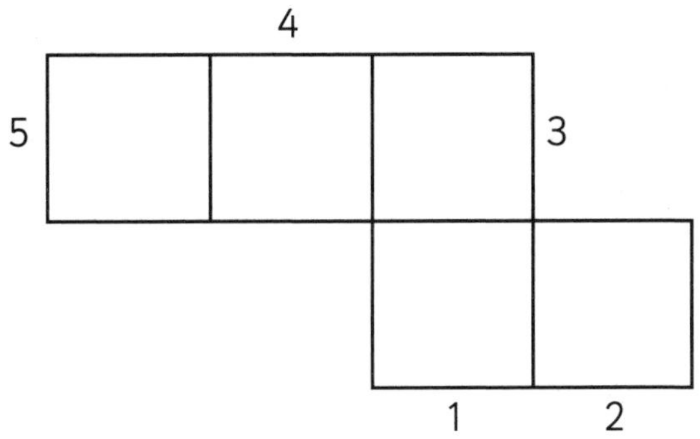

8 Gemma constructs a rectangle using two equilateral triangles and two isosceles triangles. What is the size of angle x?

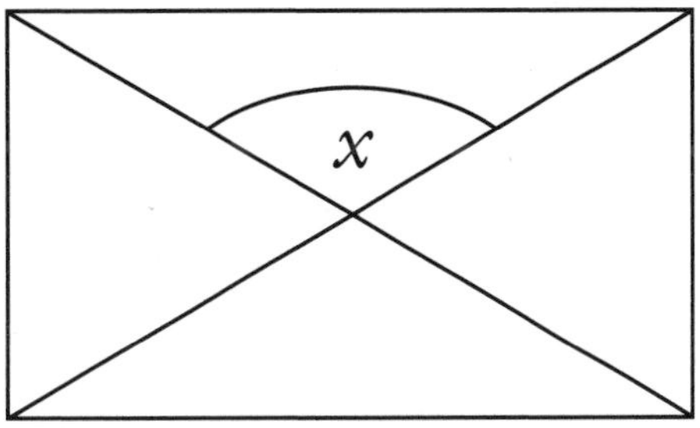

°

9 A regular hexagon has a regular square cut from its centre. How many lines of symmetry will this shape have?

10 A parallelogram is made by joining two identical rhombuses together. The length of one sloping side is given as b. What is the perimeter of the parallelogram?

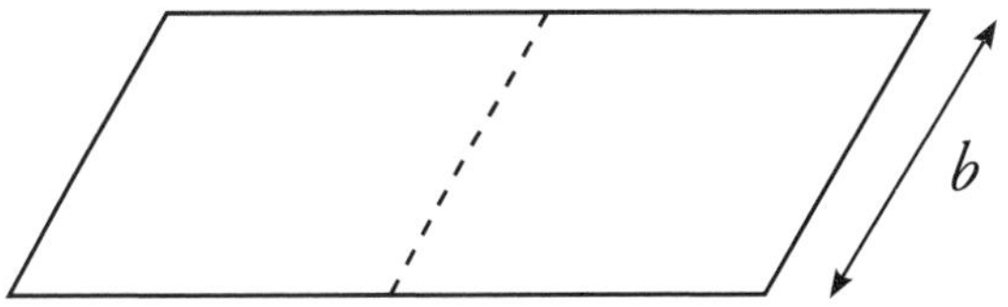

A	B	C	D	E
$4b$	$5b$	$6b$	$7b$	$8b$

/10

Data handling 1

1 There are 100 children at a tennis club. The table below shows if they are right- or left-handed. How many of the boys are right-handed?

	Girls	Boys	Total
Left-handed	4	?	7
Right-handed	?	?	?
Total	48	?	100

(boys)

2 There are 90 children at St Mary's Primary School. The pie chart below shows their mode of travel to school every day. How many children take the bus?

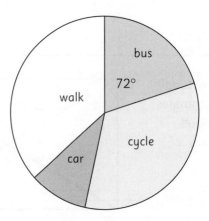

(children)

3 If 30 children cycle to school, what is the angle of the cycle sector on the pie chart?

A	B	C	D	E
80°	90°	100°	110°	120°

(   )

4 The Venn diagram shows the favourite fruits of the children in Year 6. There are 60 children altogether. How many children only like oranges?

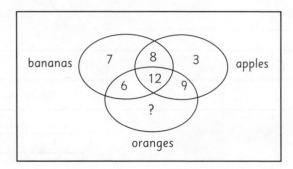

(children)

5 How many children in question 4 like any two out of the three fruits? (children)

6   Class 6 is studying Europe. They research the populations of some capital cities, presenting their data in millions.

Capital	Paris	Madrid	Rome	Berlin
Population	2.15	6.55	2.9	3.75

How many fewer people live in Paris than Rome?

$\qquad$. $\qquad$ million

---

7   The pictogram shows the mean (average) number of hours of sunshine per day from April through to September. How many hours of sunshine were there on average per day in July?

April	☼
May	☼ ☼
June	☼ ☼
July	☼ ☼ ☼ ☼
August	☼ ☼ ☼ ☼
September	☼ ☼

Key:
☼ = 3 hours

$\qquad$ hours

8   How many more hours of sunshine were there per day, on average, in August compared to April?

$\qquad$ hours

---

9   Marina makes a distance–time graph for a typical school day. She lives near to her school, and walks to and from school in the morning and afternoon, and also when she goes home for lunch.

How many minutes longer are the morning lessons than the afternoon lessons?

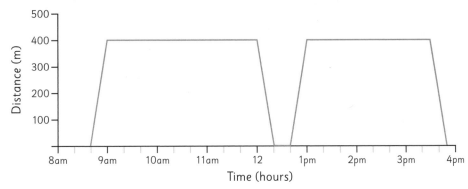

$\qquad$ minutes

---

10   A school year has 180 full days at school. If a child from Marina's school missed no days from school at all, how many hours would they be in lessons, not including lunchtimes?

A	B	C	D	E
990 hours	720 hours	1100 hours	890 hours	900 hours

/10

Data handling 2

1   The head teacher of a village school keeps a tally chart for school meals each day. Tuesday's tally is shown:

Packed lunch	⊬ℍ ⊬ℍ ⊬ℍ ⊬ℍ ⊬ℍ III
School lunch	⊬ℍ ⊬ℍ ⊬ℍ ⊬ℍ ⊬ℍ ⊬ℍ ⊬ℍ II
Going home	⊬ℍ ⊬ℍ IIII

How many children stay in school for their lunch?   (children)

---

2   The Venn diagram below shows the number of Year 5 children who own a laptop, a phone, or both. Five children do not own a phone or a laptop. If 60% of the children who currently don't have a phone or a laptop are given a phone, how many children will then own a phone?

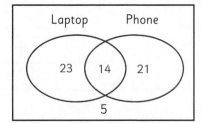

(children)

3   What proportion of children own both a laptop and a phone?

A	B	C	D	E
1 in 9	2 in 5	2 in 9	2 in 7	1 in 7

(   )

---

4   1500 people were asked to fill in a survey giving details of their favourite holiday destinations. A pie chart was created to illustrate the results.

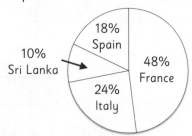

How many people preferred to holiday in France?   (people)

---

5   Jim records the maximum temperature every day at school.

Monday	Tuesday	Wednesday	Thursday	Friday
24°C	22°C	21°C	23°C	26°C

He then calculates the average temperature for the week.
What is his answer?   (. °C)

6 The chart shows data for the numbers of different people from a village that went on holiday abroad or holidayed in the United Kingdom, for three years in a row.

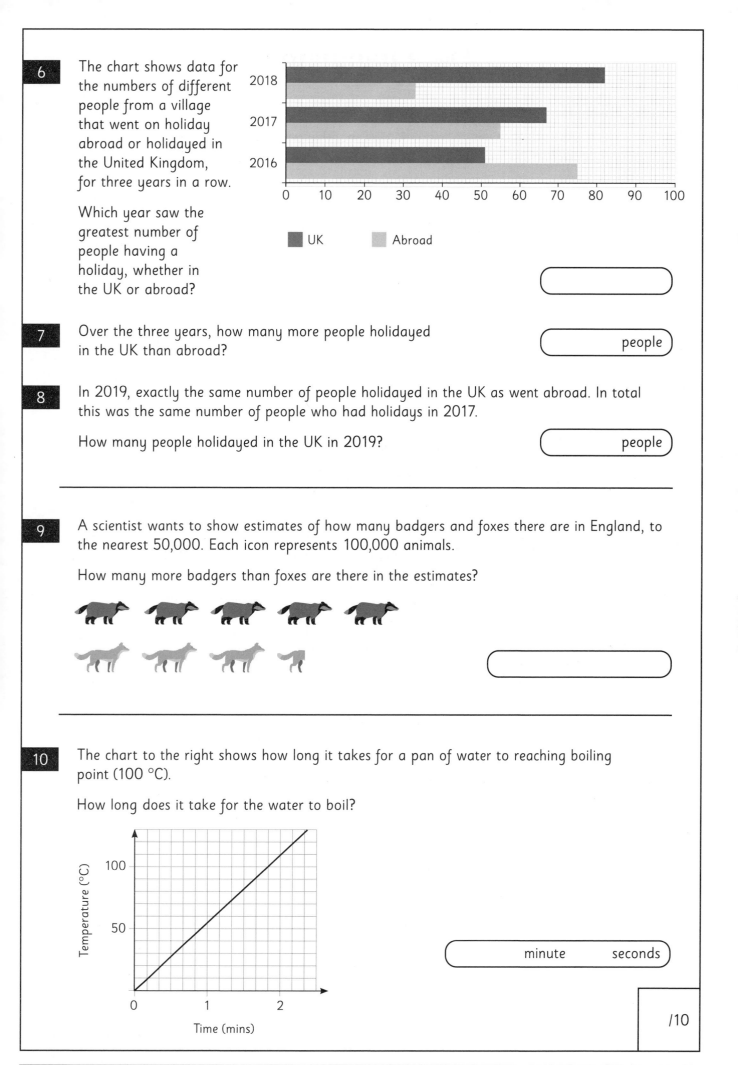

UK   Abroad

Which year saw the greatest number of people having a holiday, whether in the UK or abroad?

7 Over the three years, how many more people holidayed in the UK than abroad?

people

8 In 2019, exactly the same number of people holidayed in the UK as went abroad. In total this was the same number of people who had holidays in 2017.

How many people holidayed in the UK in 2019?

people

9 A scientist wants to show estimates of how many badgers and foxes there are in England, to the nearest 50,000. Each icon represents 100,000 animals.

How many more badgers than foxes are there in the estimates?

10 The chart to the right shows how long it takes for a pan of water to reaching boiling point (100 °C).

How long does it take for the water to boil?

minute   seconds

/10

Data handling 3

1 The chart shows the maximum and minimum monthly temperatures for Madagascar. What is the difference between the very highest and the very lowest temperature for the whole year?

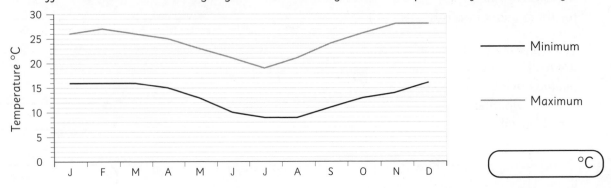

Minimum

Maximum

(°C)

2 Below is a distance chart showing the distances in kilometres between some cities in Europe. Molly drives from Rome to Milan and then on to Paris. How many kilometres has she driven?

Paris				
1420	Rome			
1275	1961	Madrid		
851	575	1577	Milan	
1735	2514	627	2133	Lisbon

(km)

3 Antoinette and Suzanna are good friends, but Antoinette lives in Paris and Suzanna lives in Madrid. They decide to meet for a holiday in Lisbon, and both of them decide to drive.

How much further does Antoinette have to drive?

A	B	C	D	E
2108km	1108km	1028km	1008km	1208km

(   )

4 180 students attending Drove Primary School were asked which their favourite subjects were. The pie chart shows the results. How many students' favourite subject was maths?

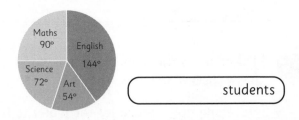

(students)

5 Jamal and Erin do a transport survey of journeys to school in their class. How many more children walk than come by all other modes of transport?

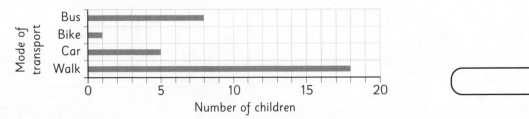

(children)

6 What percentage of children in the diagram above travel by bus? (%)

7

A teacher keeps a track of her pupils' reward points for each term of the year.

Pupil	Autumn	Spring	Summer
Adam	87	91	78
Bethan	91		81
Caitlin	76	83	86

Unfortunately, she has lost Bethan's results for the spring term. She decides that the fairest thing is to give her the mean (average) of Adam and Caitlin's points for the spring term. How many points will she give Bethan?

(points)

8

The pictogram shows the amount of rain that fell in the south-east of the country from March to September. How much more rain fell in May than in September?

 represents 12mm of rainfall.

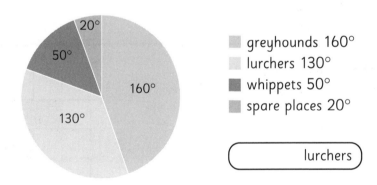

(mm)

9

A greyhound rescue centre can look after 36 dogs in total. These are shown on the pie chart.

How many lurchers are currently being looked after at the centre?

20°
50°
160°
130°

■ greyhounds 160°
■ lurchers 130°
■ whippets 50°
■ spare places 20°

(lurchers)

10

Four greyhounds and two lurchers are adopted by new owners and taken away from the rescue centre.

After the pie chart is changed, how many degrees will the 'spare places' sector be on the new pie chart?

A	B	C	D	E
6°	8°	60°	80°	100°

( )

/10

Coordinates

1   Callum is facing north. He turns 135 degrees in an anti-clockwise direction. In which direction is Callum now facing?

$\Big($ $\Big)$

2   Tina reflects point a in the y-axis, and then in the x-axis. What will be the coordinates of the new point?

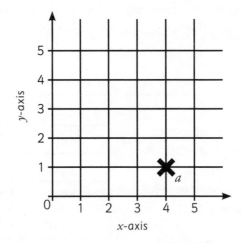

$\big($, $\big)$

3   Ahmed translates the point $(-3,-4)$ by moving it 7 along and 4 up. What are the new coordinates of the point?

A	B	C	D	E
(1,3)	(3,1)	(0,4)	(4,0)	(3,4)

$\Big($ $\Big)$

4   Simon rotates the shape below 180° anti-clockwise about its centre. What are the new coordinates of point t?

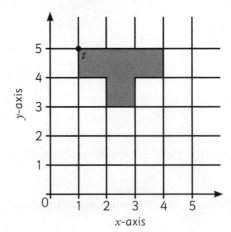

$\big($, $\big)$

5   Ashley draws a diagonal line from the coordinates (5,5) back to (0,0). He then draws a line parallel to this, starting at the point (5,3). What will be the coordinates where the second line meets the x-axis?

$\big($, $\big)$

6 A point Q has coordinates (2,1). It is reflected in the line y = 3.
What are the coordinates of the reflected point?

(,   )

---

7 The four corners of a rectangle have the following coordinates: (−3,−2), (3,−2),
(3,2) and (−3,2).

What are the coordinates of the point at the centre of the rectangle?

(,   )

---

8 Below are the coordinates of some of the features in a small town. What are the coordinates of the point exactly halfway between the gym and the cafe?

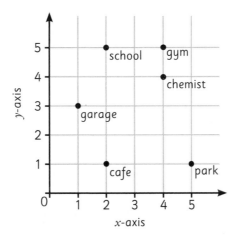

(,   )

---

9 Ali rotates the shape below 90° anti-clockwise about its centre. What are the new coordinates of point *b*?

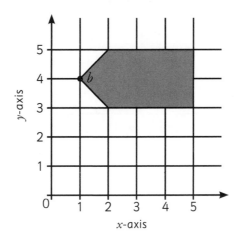

(,   )

---

10 Sarah draws a square on a coordinate grid. The bottom left-hand corner is the point (2,1), and the sides of the square are each four units long. What will be the coordinates of the top right-hand corner of the square?

A	B	C	D	E
(4,4)	(6,5)	(5,6)	(6,1)	(2,5)

/10

Algebra

1 Tom is 2kg heavier than Harry, who in turn is 3kg heavier than Ben. When they add up all their weights, it comes to 65kg.

How many kg does Harry weigh?

$\boxed{ \text{kg}}$

2 Find the value of x if $2x - 8 = 12$.

$\boxed{x = }$

3 Which formula is correct for $x = -2$ and $y = 5$?

A	B	C	D	E
$4x + 3y = 23$	$4y + 3x = 23$	$4x - 3y = 23$	$3y - 4x = 23$	$3x + 4y = 23$

$\boxed{}$

4 Will has a win on the lottery and wishes to share it among his three grandchildren, Neha, Sam and Rex. Will has won £700. He decides that he wants to give Neha twice as much as Sam, who in turn will receive twice as much as Rex. Rex decides that he will spend half and save half of his share from Grandad.

How many pounds will Rex be saving?

$\boxed{£ . }$

5 A teacher buys four extra-large bottles of water for a school trip and a pack of recyclable cups. Each cup holds 25cl of water. There are 30 children in the class, and each child drinks two cups of water. This leaves 100cl for the teacher.

Calculate how much water each bottle holds.

$\boxed{ \text{cl}}$

6 A rectangle has a perimeter of 72cm. The lengths of the longest sides are double the lengths of the shortest sides.

How long are the longest sides?

(_____ cm)

---

7 What value of y will give a value of $x = 7$ in the formula $3y + 4x = 22$?

(_____)

---

8 Josh goes to the supermarket. He buys some oranges for £1.00 each, a loaf of bread for £1.10 and a pint of milk for 80p. He receives 10p change from £10.00.

How many oranges did Josh buy?

(_____ oranges)

---

9 A teacher rewards her class with chocolate pieces at the end of each week depending on how many reward points they have received altogether. The teacher takes the total number of reward points for the class, and then divides by eight to decide how many pieces of chocolate each child is given.

One week, the class receives 56 reward points.
How many pieces of chocolate will each child receive?

(_____ pieces)

10 How many reward points would earn only two pieces of chocolate each?

(_____ points)

11 One particularly good week, the children each receive 11 pieces of chocolate.

How many reward points did they earn?

A	B	C	D	E
64	72	80	88	96

(_____)

/11

Mixed test 1

1 David has two clocks in his lounge. One is showing the time as 18:47; on the other clock, the time displayed is 19:06. One of the clocks is 11 minutes slow and the other is 8 minutes fast.

What is the correct time?

> (:)

2 Mr Taylor has started to draw a Venn diagram to show how many children in his class own a cat, a dog, both or neither.

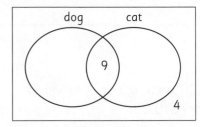

If 21 children own a dog and 12 own a cat, how many children own only a cat?

> (children)

3 Look at the scale. Which number is the arrow pointing to?

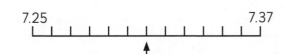

7.25   7.37

A	B	C	D	E
7.36	7.30	7.31	7.34	7.36

> (   )

4 Grace, George, Nadia and Syd are all standing for election to become Head of Year 5. 150 students voted for their favourite candidate and the results are shown in the pie chart. How many votes did Syd receive?

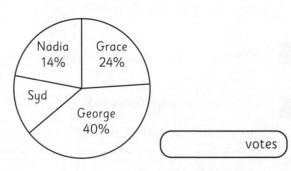

> (votes)

5 Chammi and her family are flying back from their holiday in Singapore. Singapore is 6500 miles from London and the flight takes 13 hours.

What is the average speed of the aeroplane in miles per hour?

> (mph)

6 Stephen is reading a book that has a total of 512 pages. There are 16 chapters of equal length in the book.

What are the page numbers of Chapter 12? (pages _____ to _____)

---

7 Max has four 50p coins, eight 20p coins, four 10p coins and two 2p coins. How much money does Max have in total?

(£ _____ . _____)

---

8 What percentage of the grid below has been shaded?

(_____ %)

---

9 60 passengers are on board a train when it departs from Hull. At the next station, 15 passengers leave the train and 25 board. At Leeds station, 8 passengers get off and no one boards.

How many passengers are on the train when it arrives in Bradford?

Hull   York   Leeds   Bradford

(_____ passengers)

---

10 Priya is in training to take part in the London Marathon and is running 3 kilometres every morning before breakfast and 4 kilometres every evening before dinner.

How many kilometres will Priya run over the course of a week? (_____ km)

---

11 A florist is selling bunches of flowers with eight flowers in each bunch. He sells 21 bunches in total. How many flowers does the florist sell altogether?

A	B	C	D	E
168	178	170	154	164

(_____)

/11

Mixed test 2

1 In a car park, $\frac{3}{4}$ of the cars are black. There are 240 cars in total. How many cars are colours other than black?

(cars)

2 Anna works in a cafe. This week she has been given the following amounts in tips from customers.

Monday	Tuesday	Wednesday	Thursday	Friday	Saturday	Sunday
£15.80	£12.20	£11.75	£18.30	£16.70	£20.20	£14.50

How much money has Anna made in tips in total?

(£ .)

3 Below is a timetable showing trains running from London Euston to Rugby. How many minutes does the fastest train take to travel from London to Rugby?

London Euston	Watford	Milton Keynes	Northampton	Rugby
18:33	-	19:07	19:22	19:31
18:40	18:54	19:19	-	19:40
18:46	19:01	19:13	19:24	19:39

(minutes)

4 Jamie's new baby brother, Jacob, weighed 3.24kg when he was born. In the first two weeks he gained 120g each day.

How much does Jacob weigh, in grams, after a fortnight?

(g)

5 A flight from London to New York has been overbooked by the airline and there are now more passengers than there are seats available. There are 300 seats on the plane and the flight has been overbooked by 7%. How many passengers won't be able to board the flight?

(passengers)

6

Mr Thomas's kitchen is seven and a half metres in length.
The room has an area of 30m². How wide is Mr Thomas's kitchen?

⟨ . m ⟩

7

The pictogram shows the number of tractors passing through a sleepy village in 1 week.

= Represents 15 tractors

How many fewer tractors were there in the village on Monday than on Saturday?

Monday	
Tuesday	
Wednesday	
Thursday	
Friday	
Saturday	
Sunday	

⟨ tractors ⟩

8

There are 60 children playing in a park and 15 of the children are wearing boots. What percentage of the children aren't wearing boots?

⟨ % ⟩

9

Brad is producing a movie. There are two actors starring in the leading roles and 43 other actors with parts in the movie. Brad has also organised for 240 extra actors to play small parts in the crowd scenes. In addition, there are 48 other production staff.

How many people are involved in the movie, rounded to the nearest ten?

⟨ people ⟩

10

Joe leaves his house at 08:08 to walk to school. He takes 32 minutes to get to school. His friend Neil leaves his house at 08:17 and arrives at school at 08:48. Which boy has had the longest journey?

⟨ ⟩

/10

Mixed test 3

1 An aeroplane leaves Manchester airport at 15:03 for a flight to London City airport. The flight takes 7 minutes longer than the scheduled 43 minutes. At what time does the aeroplane land at London City airport?

[:]

2 Train tickets from Bristol to Bath cost £11.75 per adult and £8.50 per child. How much will it cost for Amy and her three children to take the train to Bath?

A	B	C	D	E
£36.25	£39.75	£35.50	£37.25	£33.50

[ ]

3 Below is a floor plan of Aleksander's kitchen. What is the perimeter of the room?

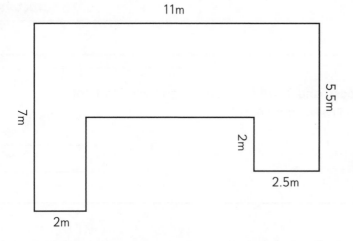

[. m]

4 Jules read the following number of pages from her book last week. What is the mean (average) number of pages that Jules reads each day?

Day	Monday	Tuesday	Wednesday	Thursday	Friday	Saturday	Sunday
Pages	34	39	27	56	42	24	30

[pages]

5 At Niagara Safari Park, there are 30 lions and 20% more elephants than lions.

How many elephants are there?

[elephants]

6 Max visits the swimming pool every other day to practise his diving. Peter swims at the same pool only on Saturdays. They meet at the pool on Saturday 1st June.

On which date will the boys next meet at the pool?

⬭

7 Elliot has made seven potions in some bottles he bought. The bottles hold 40ml, 60ml, 75ml, 25ml, 40ml, 35ml and 45ml.

What is the median of these amounts?

(ml)

8 Mr Mohamed has a newspaper delivered every morning. His Sunday newspaper costs £2.80. The other newspapers in the week all cost the same as each other. Mr Mohamed's weekly newspaper bill totals £9.40. How much does his Monday newspaper cost?

(£   .   )

9 Jenny has bought some doughnuts for the children in her class. She bought a box of 25 doughnuts and within ten minutes 40% of them have been eaten. How many doughnuts are left?

A	B	C	D	E
10	15	12	18	14

⬭

10 Workmen are relaying the tarmac on the A38. They have to resurface a total of 4km. They manage to complete 250 metres each day.

How many days will it take them to complete the resurfacing works?

(days)

11 Erica takes part in a dancing competition that begins at 18:40. She dances for 25 minutes before taking her seat to watch all the other competitors for 90 minutes. All the contestants then wait for 15 minutes before the winners are announced.

At what time are the winners announced?

(:   )

/11

Mixed test 4

1 Joshua sits an exam in which there are 60 questions. Each question is worth 1 mark. Joshua's score in the exam is 55%.

How many questions did Joshua answer incorrectly?

(questions)

2 Swati bought a t-shirt for £7.20 and paid with a £10 note. The cashier in the shop gave Swati her change in 20p coins.

How many coins did Swati receive in her change?

A	B	C	D	E
12	15	14	16	8

(   )

3 An author publishes a new book on 1st March. The chart shows the sales of the book. How many books are sold in total in the first four days of its publication?

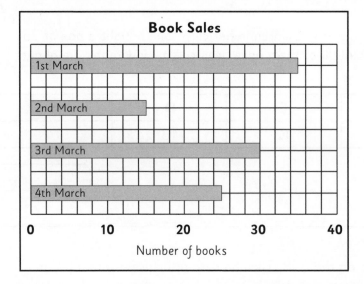

Book Sales

(books)

4 A plane flying from Heathrow to Dubai has 260 passengers on board. On the return flight, there are 20% fewer passengers.

How many passengers are there on the return flight?

(passengers)

5 Nayana buys a large bag of onions weighing 6kg and an even larger bag of potatoes weighing three times as much as the onions. How much do Nayana's vegetables weigh altogether?

Give your answer in grams.

(g)

6 A matching set of four bar stools costs £230.00.

How much would three bar stools cost?

£ _____ . ___

---

7 Samara wants to buy a new bicycle. The usual price for the bike is £140, but it has been reduced by 20% in a sale.

How much will Samara have to pay?

A	B	C	D	E
£120	£110	£108	£115	£112

(_____)

---

8 Calculate the perimeter of this shape.

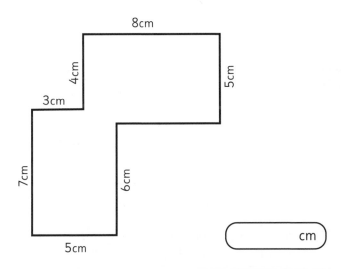

(_____ cm)

---

9 Theo's birthday falls ten days after Leo's birthday. If Leo was born on 23rd August, when is Theo's birthday?

(_____)

---

10 The graph shows the conversion rate between Thai baht (฿) and British pounds (£). How many pounds (£) would I need to exchange to get ?1200?

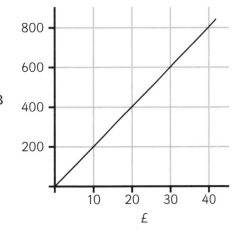

£ _____ . ___

/10

Mixed test 5

1 For every three white cars that are manufactured at a factory, there are seven black cars.

If 21 white cars are manufactured one day, how many black cars are made?

| black cars |

2 Anika puts her news jeans in the washing machine but forgets to read the washing instructions on the label first. Before she washes them, her jeans are 90cm in length. When Anika takes her jeans out of the washing machine, she is horrified to see that they have shrunk by 20%.

How long are Anika's jeans now?

| cm |

3 Joshua is having his car serviced at a garage. The service will cost £280. He also needs four new tyres at a cost of £175 each. After the work is all done, the garage adds VAT of 20% to the bill.

What is the total amount that Joshua will have to pay?

| £ . |

4 Two friends are walking on the hills in a northerly direction. After checking their map, they realise that they are travelling in completely the wrong direction. They turn 135 degrees anti-clockwise and continue walking.

In which direction are they now travelling?

A	B	C	D	E
south-west	west	south	east	north-east

| |

5 Archie and Maya manage to collect a total of £336 for charity. Archie collected £24 more than Maya.

How much money did Maya collect?

| £ . |

6 Anushka typed a number into the calculator on her phone. She multiplied this number by 3 and then added 7. The display showed the answer 142.

What was the number that Anushka first entered?

| |

7 Toby's bookshelf is 57cm long. He has a set of books on dinosaurs which are each 2.5cm thick.

How many of these books can Toby fit on his bookshelf?

books

---

8 Harry owns a newspaper shop. He sells 82 newspapers on Thursday, 79 on Friday and 89 on Saturday. The total for these three days is still 48 fewer than the number of newspapers that Harry sells on Sunday.

How many newspapers does Harry sell on Sunday?

A	B	C	D	E
248	272	288	298	308

---

9 $\frac{5}{8}$ of people who completed a survey said that they preferred to watch movies at home rather than at the cinema. If 72 people completed the survey, how many people preferred to watch movies at the cinema?

people

---

10 Farmer Cole wants to replace the fence around his rectangular field. The shorter side of the field is 11 metres long and the other side is 26 metres long.

How many metres of fencing will farmer Cole need to buy?

metres

---

11 Stella's flight home from her holiday in India took off at 09:00. Mumbai is $5\frac{1}{2}$ hours ahead of London. She lands safely in London where the local time is 13:30.

How long did Stella's flight take?

hours

---

12 Lewis, his older brother Erik and his sister Annie clean their mother's car. Their mother hands over £7.50 to share equally between them. Lewis also mows the lawn and is given £3.50 for this extra chore.

How much has Lewis earned?

A	B	C	D	E
£6.25	£6.00	£5.75	£7.00	£5.75

/12

Answers

Extended answers with useful explanations are available online at **www.scholastic.co.uk/pass-your-11-plus/extras** or via the QR code.

Properties of numbers
pp.6–7

1	3917
2	7 hundred thousand
3	D
4	2 hundred thousand
5	24
6	–2°C
7	31,000 supporters
8	95
9	–7°C
10	5
11	5

Addition and subtraction
pp.8–9

1	146,325
2	16,600 vegetables
3	C
4	10p
5	243,000
6	333
7	£17,775.00
8	1,400,000
9	2158kg
10	2146
11	E

Multiplication and division
pp.10–11

1	135 pages
2	D
3	3 sweets
4	£61.00
5	18 sheets of paper
6	4
7	28 children
8	15
9	£5000.00
10	100m
11	D

Time
pp.12–13

1	13:20
2	1st March
3	B
4	2 hours 30 minutes
5	14:20
6	7 hours 30 minutes
7	7 hours 32 minutes
8	4 hours 18 minutes
9	17th March
10	113 hours
11	A

Money 1
pp.14–15

1	7 coins
2	32 packs
3	E
4	£1.52
5	£180.00
6	28 coins
7	£1332.00
8	£252.00
9	£9.00
10	B

Money 2
pp.16–17

1	£67.50
2	£200,000.00
3	B
4	6000 Egyptian pounds
5	£88.00
6	£42.00
7	£525.40
8	¥75,000
9	£720.00
10	A

Fractions
pp.18–19

1	8474 spectators
2	20 children
3	D
4	25 children
5	54 balloons
6	16 chocolates
7	816kg
8	£6.00
9	27 litres
10	26 eggs
11	40 cakes
12	A

Decimals
pp.20–21

1	0.04
2	34.8cm
3	D
4	30m
5	27.94cm
6	3.65g
7	0.735kg
8	4000 grains of rice
9	22.8 litres
10	B

Percentages
pp.22–23

1	440 girls
2	£300,000.00
3	E
4	2 questions
5	15%
6	£21.00
7	20%
8	306 miles
9	200 students
10	£3200.00
11	B

Ratio
pp.24–25

1	20°
2	12 sweets
3	C
4	800m
5	£45.00
6	D
7	£16.80
8	30 boys
9	125g
10	1006 books
11	B

Proportion
pp.26–27

1	£16.20
2	28 bunches
3	A
4	55g
5	6 girls
6	150 vehicles
7	4 racehorses
8	3 eggs
9	36 litres
10	2 litres
11	450g
12	B

Probability
pp.28–29

1	2 in 3
2	13 yellow marbles
3	B
4	5 in 8
5	12 counters
6	35 chocolates
7	2 red handkerchiefs
8	9 in 10
9	3 in 4
10	5 in 13
11	C

Area and perimeter
pp.30–31

1	128 tiles
2	36mm²
3	B
4	9 boxes
5	24m²
6	54m²
7	69.2m
8	12cm
9	32cm
10	A

Statistics
p.32–33

1	44
2	11 years old
3	A
4	26mm
5	43 years old
6	20°C
7	11
8	21°C
9	3 minutes 22 seconds
10	8 minutes 19 seconds
11	D

Measurement
pp.34–35

1	270,000cm
2	250g
3	E
4	54,000 seconds
5	75 miles
6	0.4lb
7	3 litres
8	12 cubes
9	175 hours
10	B

Speed, distance and time
pp.36–37

1	6mph
2	3360 miles
3	A
4	790m
5	6 metres per second
6	10 minutes
7	4 hours
8	660km
9	60 seconds
10	E

Geometry 1
pp.38–39

1	80°
2	118°
3	B
4	225°
5	8 vertices
6	60°
7	150°
8	12cm
9	65°
10	51cm
11	C

Geometry 2
pp.40–41

1	cuboid
2	210°
3	30°
4	14cm
5	30°
6	12 edges
7	4
8	120°
9	2
10	C

Data handling 1
pp.42–43

1	49 boys
2	18 children
3	E
4	15 children
5	23 children
6	0.75 million
7	12 hours
8	9 hours
9	30 minutes
10	A

Data handling 2
pp.44–45

1	65 children
2	38 children
3	C
4	720 people
5	23.2°C
6	2016
7	37 people
8	61 people
9	150,000
10	1 minute and 50 seconds

Data handling 3
pp.46–47

1	19°C
2	1426km
3	B
4	45 students
5	4 children
6	25%
7	87 points
8	60mm
9	13 lurchers
10	D

Coordinates
pp. 48–49

1	southwest
2	(–4,–1)
3	D
4	(4,3)
5	(0,2)
6	(2,5)
7	(0,0)
8	(3,3)
9	(3,2)
10	B

Algebra
pp. 50–51

1	22kg
2	$x = 10$
3	D
4	£50.00
5	400cl
6	24cm
7	–2
8	8 oranges
9	7 pieces
10	16 points
11	D

Mixed test 1
pp.52–53

1	18:58
2	3 children
3	C
4	33 votes
5	500mph
6	pages 353 to 384
7	£4.04
8	64%
9	62 passengers
10	49km
11	A

Mixed test 2
pp.54–55

1	60 cars
2	£109.45
3	53 minutes
4	4920g
5	21 passengers
6	4.0m
7	30 tractors
8	75%
9	330 people
10	Joe

Mixed test 3
pp.56–57

1	15:53
2	D
3	40m
4	36 pages
5	36 elephants
6	Saturday 15th June
7	40ml
8	£1.10
9	B
10	16 days
11	20:50

Mixed test 4
pp.58–59

1	27 questions
2	C
3	105 books
4	208 passengers
5	24,000g
6	£172.50
7	E
8	44cm
9	2nd September
10	£60,00

Mixed test 5
pp.60–61

1	49 black cars
2	72cm
3	£1176.00
4	B
5	£156.00
6	45
7	22 books
8	D
9	27 people
10	74 metres
11	10 hours
12	B